The Death
Notebooks

Anne Sexton

The Death Notebooks

HOUGHTON MIFFLIN COMPANY BOSTON

1974

Some of the poems in this book have appeared in
American Poetry Review, Boston University Journal,
The Castalian, Kayak, Salmagundi, and *Saturday*
Review.

"Overshoes" and "Grandfather, Your Wound" originally
appeared in *The New Yorker.* "Praying on a 707"
originally appeared in *The Atlantic.*

First Printing   v

Library of Congress Cataloging in Publication Data
Sexton, Anne.
  The death notebooks.
  Poems.
  I. Title.
PS3537.E915D4   811'.5'4   73–17311
  ISBN 0–395–18281–6

Printed in the United States of America

Because of mirrors
And mashed potatoes
for
Louise and Loring

"Look, you con man, make a living
out of your death."

ERNEST HEMINGWAY,
A *Moveable Feast*

CONTENTS

The Death
Notebooks

GODS

Mrs. Sexton went out looking for the gods.
She began looking in the sky —
expecting a large white angel with a blue crotch.

No one.

She looked next in all the learned books
and the print spat back at her.

No one.

She made a pilgrimage to the great poet
and he belched in her face.

No one.

She prayed in all the churches of the world
and learned a great deal about culture.

No one.

She went to the Atlantic, the Pacific, for surely God . . .
No one.

She went to the Buddha, the Brahma, the Pyramids
and found immense postcards.

No one.

Then she journeyed back to her own house
and the gods of the world were shut in the lavatory.

At last!
she cried out,
and locked the door.

MAKING A LIVING

Jonah made his living
inside the belly.
Mine comes from the exact same place.
Jonah opened the door of his stateroom
and said, "Here I am!" and the whale liked this
and thought to take him in.

At the mouth Jonah cried out.
At the stomach he was humbled.
He did not beat on the walls.
Nor did he suck his thumb.
He cocked his head attentively
like a defendant at his own trial.

Jonah took out the wallet of his father
and tried to count the money
and it was all washed away.
Jonah took out the picture of his mother
and tried to kiss the eyes
and it was all washed away.
Jonah took off his coat and his trousers,
his tie, his watch fob, his cuff links
and gave them up.
He sat like an old-fashioned bather
in his undershirt and drawers.

This is my death,
Jonah said out loud,

and it will profit me to understand it.
I will make a mental note of each detail.
Little fish swam by his nose
and he noted them and touched their slime.
Plankton came and he held them in his palm
like God's littlest light bulbs.
His whole past was there with him
and he ate that.

At this point the whale
vomited him back out into the sea.
The shocking blue sky.
The shocking white boats.
The sun like a crazed eyeball.
Then he told the news media
the strange details of his death
and they hammered him up in the marketplace
and sold him and sold him and sold him.
My death the same.

FOR MR. DEATH WHO STANDS WITH HIS DOOR OPEN

Time grows dim. Time that was so long
grows short, time, all goggle-eyed,
wiggling her skirts, singing her torch song,
giving the boys a buzz and a ride,
that Nazi Mama with her beer and sauerkraut.
Time, old gal of mine, will soon dim out.

May I say how young she was back then,
playing piggley-witch and hoola-hoop,
dancing the jango with six awful men,
letting the chickens out of the coop,
promising to marry Jack and Jerome,
and never bothering, never, never,
to come back home.

Time was when time had time enough
and the sea washed me daily in its delicate brine.
There is no terror when you swim in the buff
or speed up the boat and hang out a line.
Time was when I could hiccup and hold my breath
and not in that instant meet Mr. Death.

Mr. Death, you actor, you have many masks.
Once you were sleek, a kind of Valentino
with my father's bathtub gin in your flask.
With my cinched-in waist and my dumb vertigo

at the crook of your long white arm
and yet you never bent me back, never, never,
into your blackguard charm.

Next, Mr. Death, you held out the bait
during my first decline, as they say,
telling that suicide baby to celebrate
her own going in her own puppet play.
I went out popping pills and crying adieu
in my own death camp with my own little Jew.

Now your beer belly hangs out like Fatso.
You are popping your buttons and expelling gas.
How can I lie down with you, my comical beau
when you are so middle-aged and lower-class.
Yet you'll press me down in your envelope;
pressed as neat as a butterfly, forever, forever,
beside Mussolini and the Pope.

Mr. Death, when you came to the ovens it was short
and to the drowning man you were likewise kind,
and the nicest of all to the baby I had to abort
and middling you were to all the crucified combined.
But when it comes to my death let it be slow,
let it be pantomine, this last peep show,
so that I may squat at the edge trying on
my black necessary trousseau.

FAUSTUS AND I

I went to the opera and God was not there.
I was, at the time, in my apprenticeship.
The voices were as full as goblets; in mid-air
I caught them and threw them back. A form of worship.
In those vacant moments when our Lord sleeps
I have the voices. A cry that is mine for keeps.

I went to the galleries and God was not there,
only Mother Roulin and her baby, an old man infant,
his face lined in black and with a strange stare
in his black, black eyes. They seemed to hunt
me down. At the gallery van Gogh was violent
as the crows in the wheat field began their last ascent.

Three roads led to that death. All of them blind.
The sky had the presence of a thousand blue eyes
and the wheat beat itself. The wheat was not kind.
The crows go up immediately like an old man's lies.
The crimes, my Dutchman, that wait within us all
crawled out of that sea long before the fall.

I went to the bookstore and God was not there.
Doctor Faustus was baby blue with a Knopf dog
on his spine. He was frayed and threadbare
with needing. The arch-deceiver and I had a dialogue.
The Debble and I, the Father of Lies himself,
communed, as it were, from the bookshelf.

I have made a pact and a half in my day
and stolen Godes Boke during a love affair,
the Gideon itself for all devout salesmen who pray.
The Song of Solomon was underlined by some earlier pair.
The rest of the words turned to wood in my hands.
I am not immortal. Faustus and I are the also-ran.

THE DEATH BABY

THE DEATH BABY

1. Dreams

I was an ice baby.
I turned to sky blue.
My tears became two glass beads.
My mouth stiffened into a dumb howl.
They say it was a dream
but I remember that hardening.

My sister at six
dreamt nightly of my death:
"The baby turned to ice.
Someone put her in the refrigerator
and she turned as hard as a Popsicle."

I remember the stink of the liverwurst.
How I was put on a platter and laid
between the mayonnaise and the bacon.
The rhythm of the refrigerator
had been disturbed.
The milk bottle hissed like a snake.
The tomatoes vomited up their stomachs.
The caviar turned to lava.
The pimentos kissed like cupids.
I moved like a lobster,
slower and slower.

The air was tiny.
The air would not do.

＊

I was at the dogs' party.
I was their bone.
I had been laid out in their kennel
like a fresh turkey.
This was my sister's dream
but I remember that quartering;
I remember the sickbed smell
of the sawdust floor, the pink eyes,
the pink tongues and the teeth, those nails.
I had been carried out like Moses
and hidden by the paws
of ten Boston bull terriers,
ten angry bulls
jumping like enormous roaches.
At first I was lapped,
rough as sandpaper.
I became very clean.
Then my arm was missing.
I was coming apart.
They loved me until
I was gone.

2. The Dy-dee Doll

My Dy-dee doll
died twice.

To beat death down with a stick.
To take over.
To build our death like carpenters.
When she had a broken back,
each night we built her sleep.
Talking on the hot line
until her eyes pulled down like shades.
And we agreed in those long hushed phone calls
that when the moment comes
we'll talk turkey,
we'll shoot words straight from the hip,
we'll play it as it lays.
Yes,
when death comes with its hood
we won't be polite.

6. Baby

Death,
you lie in my arms like a cherub,
as heavy as bread dough.
Your milky wings are as still as plastic.
Hair as soft as music.
Hair the color of a harp.
And eyes made of glass,
as brittle as crystal.
Each time I rock you
I think you will break.
I rock. I rock.
Glass eye, ice eye,

primordial eye,
lava eye,
pin eye,
break eye,
how you stare back!

Like the gaze of small children
you know all about me.
You have worn my underwear.
You have read my newspaper.
You have seen my father whip me.
You have seen me stroke my father's whip.

I rock. I rock.
We plunge back and forth
comforting each other.
We are stone.
We are carved, a pietà
that swings and swings.
Outside, the world is a chilly army.
Outside, the sea is brought to its knees.
Outside, Pakistan is swallowed in a mouthful.

I rock. I rock.
You are my stone child
with still eyes like marbles.
There is a death baby
for each of us.
We own him.
His smell is our smell.
Beware. Beware.
There is a tenderness.

There is a love
for this dumb traveler
waiting in his pink covers.
Someday,
heavy with cancer or disaster
I will look up at Max
and say: It is time.
Hand me the death baby
and there will be
that final rocking.

RATS LIVE ON NO EVIL STAR

A palindrome seen on the side of a barn in Ireland

After Adam broke his rib in two
and ate it for supper,
after Adam, from the waist up,
an old mother,
had begun to question the wonder
Eve was brought forth.
Eve came out of that rib like an angry bird.
She came forth like a bird that got loose
suddenly from its cage.
Out of the cage came Eve,
escaping, escaping.
She was clothed in her skin like the sun
and her ankles were not for sale.

God looked out through his tunnel
and was pleased.

Adam sat like a lawyer
and read the book of life.
Only his eyes were alive.
They did the work of a blast furnace.

Only later did Adam and Eve go galloping,
galloping into the apple.
They made the noise of the moon-chew
and let the juice fall down like tears.

Because of this same apple
Eve gave birth to the evilest of creatures
with its bellyful of dirt
and its hair seven inches long.
It had two eyes full of poison
and routine pointed teeth.
Thus Eve gave birth.
In this unnatural act
she gave birth to a rat.
It slid from her like a pearl.
It was ugly, of course,
but Eve did not know that
and when it died before its time
she placed its tiny body
on that piece of kindergarten called STAR.

Now all us cursed ones falling out after
with our evil mouths and our worried eyes
die before our time
but do not go to some heaven, some hell
but are put on the RAT'S STAR
which is as wide as Asia
and as happy as a barbershop quartet.
We are put there beside the three thieves
for the lowest of us all
deserve to smile in eternity
like a watermelon.

GRANDFATHER, YOUR WOUND

The wound is open,
Grandfather, where you died,
where you sit inside it
as shy as a robin.
I am an ocean-going vessel
but you are a ceiling made of wood
and the island you were the man of,
is shaped like a squirrel and named thereof.
On this island, Grandfather, made of your stuff,
a rubber squirrel sits on the kitchen table
coughing up mica like phlegm.

I stand in your writing room
with the Atlantic painting its way toward us
and ask why am I left with stuffed fish on the wall,
why am I left with rubber squirrels with mica eyes,
when you were Mr. Funnyman, Mr. Nativeman,
when you were Mr. Lectureman, Mr. Editor,
the small town big shot who, although very short,
who although with a cigarette-stained mustache,
who although famous for lobster on the rocks,
left me here, nubkin, sucking in my vodka
and emphysema cigarettes, unable to walk
your walks, unable to write your writes.

Grandfather,
you blow your bone like a horn

and I hear it inside my pink facecloth.
I hear you, Mr. Iodineman,
and the sun goes down
just as it did in your life,
like a campaign ribbon,
an ingot from the iron works,
an eyelash,
and a dot and a dash.
Now it comes bright again —
my God, Grandfather,
you are here,
you are laughing,
you hold me and rock me
and we watch the lighthouse come on,
blinking its dry wings over us all,
over my wound
and yours.

BABY PICTURE

It's in the heart of the grape
where that smile lies.
It's in the good-bye-bow in the hair
where that smile lies.
It's in the clerical collar of the dress
where that smile lies.
What smile?
The smile of my seventh year,
caught here in the painted photograph.

It's peeling now, age has got it,
a kind of cancer of the background
and also in the assorted features.
It's like a rotten flag
or a vegetable from the refrigerator,
pocked with mold.
I am aging without sound,
into darkness, darkness.

Anne,
who were you?

I open the vein
and my blood rings like roller skates.
I open the mouth
and my teeth are an angry army.

I open the eyes
and they go sick like dogs
with what they have seen.
I open the hair
and it falls apart like dust balls.
I open the dress
and I see a child bent on a toilet seat.
I crouch there, sitting dumbly
pushing the enemas out like ice cream,
letting the whole brown world
turn into sweets.

Anne,
who were you?

Merely a kid keeping alive.

THE FURIES

THE FURY OF BEAUTIFUL BONES

Sing me a thrush, bone.
Sing me a nest of cup and pestle.
Sing me a sweetbread for an old grandfather.
Sing me a foot and a doorknob, for you are my love.
Oh sing, bone bag man, sing.
Your head is what I remember that August,
you were in love with another woman but
that didn't matter. I was the fury of your
bones, your fingers long and nubby, your
forehead a beacon, bare as marble and I worried
you like an odor because you had not quite forgotten,
bone bag man, garlic in the North End,
the book you dedicated, naked as a fish,
naked as someone drowning into his own mouth.
I wonder, Mr. Bone man, what you're thinking
of your fury now, gone sour as a sinking whale,
crawling up the alphabet on her own bones.
Am I in your ear still singing songs in the rain,
me of the death rattle, me of the magnolias,
me of the sawdust tavern at the city's edge.
Women have lovely bones, arms, neck, thigh
and I admire them also, but your bones
supersede loveliness. They are the tough
ones that get broken and reset. I just can't
answer for you, only for your bones,
round rulers, round nudgers, round poles,

numb nubkins, the sword of sugar.
I feel the skull, Mr. Skeleton, living its
own life in its own skin.

THE FURY OF HATING EYES

I would like to bury
all the hating eyes
under the sand somewhere off
the North Atlantic and suffocate
them with the awful sand
and put all their colors to sleep
in that soft smother.
Take the brown eyes of my father,
those gun shots, those mean muds.
Bury them.
Take the blue eyes of my mother,
naked as the sea,
waiting to pull you down
where there is no air, no God.
Bury them.
Take the black eyes of my lover,
coal eyes like a cruel hog,
wanting to whip you and laugh.
Bury them.
Take the hating eyes of martyrs,
presidents, bus collectors,
bank managers, soldiers.
Bury them.
Take my eyes, half blind
and falling into the air.
Bury them.

Take your eyes.
I come to the center,
where a shark looks up at death
and thinks of my death.
They'd like to take my heart
and squeeze it like a doughnut.
They'd like to take my eyes
and poke a hatpin through
their pupils. Not just to bury
but to stab. As for your eyes,
I fold up in front of them
in a baby ball and you send
them to the State Asylum.
Look! Look! Both those
mice are watching you
from behind the kind bars.

THE FURY OF GUITARS
AND SOPRANOS

This singing
is a kind of dying,
a kind of birth,
a votive candle.
I have a dream-mother
who sings with her guitar,
nursing the bedroom
with moonlight and beautiful olives.
A flute came too,
joining the five strings,
a God finger over the holes.
I knew a beautiful woman once
who sang with her fingertips
and her eyes were brown
like small birds.
At the cup of her breasts
I drew wine.
At the mound of her legs
I drew figs.
She sang for my thirst,
mysterious songs of God
that would have laid an army down.
It as as if a morning-glory
had bloomed in her throat

and all that blue
and small pollen
ate into my heart
violent and religious.

THE FURY OF EARTH

The day of fire is coming, the thrush
will fly ablaze like a little sky rocket,
the beetle will sink like a giant bulldozer,
and at the breaking of the morning the houses
will turn into oil and will in their tides
of fire be a becoming and an ending, a red fan.
What then, man in your easy chair,
of the anointment of the sick,
of the New Jerusalem?
You will have to polish up the stars
with Bab-o and find a new God
as the earth empties out
into the gnarled hands of the old redeemer.

THE FURY OF JEWELS AND COAL

Many a miner has gone
into the deep pit
to receive the dust of a kiss,
an ore-cell.
He has gone with his lamp
full of mole eyes
deep deep and has brought forth
Jesus at Gethsemane.
Body of moss, body of glass,
body of peat, how sharp
you lie, emerald as heavy
as a golf course, ruby as dark
as an afterbirth,
diamond as white as sun
on the sea, coal, dark mother,
brood mother, let the sea birds
bring you into our lives
as from a distant island,
heavy as death.

THE FURY OF COOKS

Herbs, garlic,
cheese, please let me in!
Souffles, salads,
Parker House rolls,
please let me in!
Cook Helen,
why are you so cross,
why is your kitchen verboten?
Couldn't you just teach me
to bake a potato,
that charm,
that young prince?
No! No!
This is my country!
You shout silently.
Couldn't you just show me
the gravy. How you drill it out
of the stomach of that bird?
Helen, Helen,
let me in,
let me feel the flour,
is it blind and frightening,
this stuff that makes cakes?
Helen, Helen,
the kitchen is your dog
and you pat it

and love it
and keep it clean.
But all these things,
all these dishes of things
come through the swinging door
and I don't know from where?
Give me some tomato aspic, Helen!
I don't want to be alone.

THE FURY OF COCKS

There they are
drooping over the breakfast plates,
angel-like,
folding in their sad wing,
animal sad,
and only the night before
there they were
playing the banjo.
Once more the day's light comes
with its immense sun,
its mother trucks,
its engines of amputation.
Whereas last night
the cock knew its way home,
as stiff as a hammer,
battering in with all
its awful power.
That theater.
Today it is tender,
a small bird,
as soft as a baby's hand.
She is the house.
He is the steeple.
When they fuck they are God.
When they break away they are God.
When they snore they are God.

In the morning they butter the toast.
They don't say much.
They are still God.
All the cocks of the world are God,
blooming, blooming, blooming
into the sweet blood of woman.

THE FURY OF ABANDONMENT

Someone lives in a cave
eating his toes,
I know that much.
Someone little lives under a bush
pressing an empty Coca-Cola can against
his starving bloated stomach,
I know that much.
A monkey had his hands cut off
for a medical experiment
and his claws wept.
I know that much.

I know that it is all
a matter of hands.
Out of the mournful sweetness of touching
comes love
like breakfast.
Out of the many houses come the hands
before the abandonment of the city,
out of the bars and shops,
a thin file of ants.

I've been abandoned out here
under the dry stars
with no shoes, no belt
and I've called Rescue Inc. —

that old-fashioned hot line —
no voice.
Left to my own lips, touch them,
my own dumb eyes, touch them,
the progression of my parts, touch them,
my own nostrils, shoulders, breasts,
navel, stomach, mound, kneebone, ankle,
touch them.

It makes me laugh
to see a woman in this condition.
It makes me laugh for America and New York City
when your hands are cut off
and no one answers the phone.

THE FURY OF OVERSHOES

They sit in a row
outside the kindergarten,
black, red, brown, all
with those brass buckles.
Remember when you couldn't
buckle your own
overshoe
or tie your own
shoe
or cut your own meat
and the tears
running down like mud
because you fell off your
tricycle?
Remember, big fish,
when you couldn't swim
and simply slipped under
like a stone frog?
The world wasn't
yours.
It belonged to
the big people.
Under your bed
sat the wolf
and he made a shadow
when cars passed by

at night.
They made you give up
your nightlight
and your teddy
and your thumb.
Oh overshoes,
don't you
remember me,
pushing you up and down
in the winter snow?
Oh thumb,
I want a drink,
it is dark,
where are the big people,
when will I get there,
taking giant steps
all day,
each day
and thinking
nothing of it?

THE FURY OF RAIN STORMS

The rain drums down like red ants,
each bouncing off my window.
These ants are in great pain
and they cry out as they hit,
as if their little legs were only
stitched on and their heads pasted.
And oh they bring to mind the grave,
so humble, so willing to be beat upon
with its awful lettering and
the body lying underneath
without an umbrella.

Depression is boring, I think,
and I would do better to make
some soup and light up the cave.

THE FURY OF FLOWERS AND WORMS

Let the flowers make a journey
on Monday so that I can see
ten daisies in a blue vase
with perhaps one red ant
crawling to the gold center.
A bit of the field on my table,
close to the worms
who struggle blindly,
moving deep into their slime,
moving deep into God's abdomen,
moving like oil through water,
sliding through the good brown.

The daisies grow wild
like popcorn.
They are God's promise to the field.
How happy I am, daisies, to love you.
How happy you are to be loved
and found magical, like a secret
from the sluggish field.
If all the world picked daisies
wars would end, the common cold would stop,
unemployment would end, the monetary market
would hold steady and no money would float.

Listen world,
if you'd just take the time to pick

the white fingers, the penny heart,
all would be well.
They are so unexpected.
They are as good as salt.
If someone had brought them
to van Gogh's room daily
his ear would have stayed on.
I would like to think that no one would die anymore
if we all believed in daisies
but the worms know better, don't they?
They slide into the ear of a corpse
and listen to his great sigh.

THE FURY OF GOD'S GOOD-BYE

One day He
tipped His top hat
and walked
out of the room,
ending the argument.
He stomped off
saying:
I don't give guarantees.
I was left
quite alone
using up the darkness.
I rolled up
my sweater,
up into a ball,
and took it
to bed with me,
a kind of stand-in
for God,
that washerwoman
who walks out
when you're clean
but not ironed.

When I woke up
the sweater
had turned to

bricks of gold.
I'd won the world
but like a
forsaken explorer,
I'd lost
my map.

THE FURY OF SUNDAYS

Moist, moist,
the heat leaking through the hinges,
sun baking the roof like a pie
and I and thou and she
eating, working, sweating,
droned up on the heat.
The sun as red as the cop car siren.
The sun as red as the algebra marks.
The sun as red as two electric eyeballs.
She wanting to take a bath in jello.
You and me sipping vodka and soda,
ice cubes melting like the Virgin Mary.
You cutting the lawn, fixing the machines,
all this leprous day and then more vodka,
more soda and the pond forgiving our bodies,
the pond sucking out the throb.
Our bodies were trash.
We leave them on the shore.
I and thou and she
swim like minnows,
losing all our queens and kings,
losing our heels and our tongues,
cool, cool, all day that Sunday in July
when we were young and did not look
into the abyss,
that God spot.

THE FURY OF SUNSETS

Something
cold is in the air,
an aura of ice
and phlegm.
All day I've built
a lifetime and now
the sun sinks to
undo it.
The horizon bleeds
and sucks its thumb.
The little red thumb
goes out of sight.
And I wonder about
this lifetime with myself,
this dream I'm living.
I could eat the sky
like an apple
but I'd rather
ask the first star:
why am I here?
why do I live in this house?
who's responsible?
eh?

THE FURY OF SUNRISES

Darkness
as black as your eyelid,
poketricks of stars,
the yellow mouth,
the smell of a stranger,
dawn coming up,
dark blue,
no stars,
the smell of a lover,
warmer now
as authentic as soap,
wave after wave
of lightness
and the birds in their chains
going mad with throat noises,
the birds in their tracks
yelling into their cheeks like clowns,
lighter, lighter,
the stars gone,
the trees appearing in their green hoods,
the house appearing across the way,
the road and its sad macadam,
the rock walls losing their cotton,
lighter, lighter,
letting the dog out and seeing
fog lift by her legs,

a gauze dance,
lighter, lighter,
yellow, blue at the tops of trees,
more God, more God everywhere,
lighter, lighter,
more world everywhere,
sheets bent back for people,
the strange heads of love
and breakfast,
that sacrament,
lighter, yellower,
like the yolk of eggs,
the flies gathering at the windowpane,
the dog inside whining for food
and the day commencing,
not to die, not to die,
as in the last day breaking,
a final day digesting itself,
lighter, lighter,
the endless colors,
the same old trees stepping toward me,
the rock unpacking its crevices,
breakfast like a dream
and the whole day to live through,
steadfast, deep, interior.
After the death,
after the black of black,
this lightness —
not to die, not to die —
that God begot.

PRAYING ON A 707

Mother,
each time I talk to God
you interfere.
You of the bla-bla set,
carrying on about the state of letters.
If I write a poem
you give a treasurer's report.
If I make love
you give me the funniest lines.
Mrs. Sarcasm,
why are there any children left?

They hold up their bows.
They curtsy in just your style.
They shake hands how-do-you-do
in the same inimitable manner.
They pass over the soup with parsley
as you never could.
They take their children into their arms
like cups of warm cocoa
as you never could
and yet and yet
with your smile, your dimple we ape you,
we ape you further . . .
the great pine of summer,
the beach that oiled you,

the garden made of noses,
the moon tied down over the sea,
the great warm-blooded dogs . . .
the doll you gave me, Mary Gray,
or your mother gave me
or the maid gave me.
Perhaps the maid.
She had soul,
being Italian.

Mother,
each time I talk to God
you interfere.
Up there in the jet,
below the clouds as small as puppies,
the sun standing fire,
I talk to God and ask Him
to speak of my failures, my successes,
ask Him to morally make an assessment.
He does.

He says,
you haven't,
you haven't.

Mother,
you and God
float with the same belly
up.

CLOTHES

Put on a clean shirt
before you die, some Russian said.
Nothing with drool, please,
no egg spots, no blood,
no sweat, no sperm.
You want me clean, God,
so I'll try to comply.

The hat I was married in,
will it do?
White, broad, fake flowers in a tiny array.
It's old-fashioned, as stylish as a bedbug,
but it suits to die in something nostalgic.

And I'll take
my painting shirt
washed over and over of course
spotted with every yellow kitchen I've painted.
God, you don't mind if I bring all my kitchens?
They hold the family laughter and the soup.

For a bra
(need we mention it?),
the padded black one that my lover demeaned
when I took it off.
He said, "Where'd it all go?"

And I'll take
the maternity skirt of my ninth month,
a window for the love-belly
that let each baby pop out like an apple,
the water breaking in the restaurant,
making a noisy house I'd like to die in.

For underpants I'll pick white cotton,
the briefs of my childhood,
for it was my mother's dictum
that nice girls wore only white cotton.
If my mother had lived to see it
she would have put a WANTED sign up in the post office
for the black, the red, the blue I've worn.
Still, it would be perfectly fine with me
to die like a nice girl
smelling of Clorox and Duz.
Being sixteen-in-the-pants
I would die full of questions.

MARY'S SONG

Out of Egypt
with its pearls and honey,
out of Abraham, Isaac, Jacob,
out of the God I AM,
out of the diseased snakes,
out of the droppings of flies,
out of the sand dry as paper,
out of the deaf blackness,
I come here to give birth.

Write these words down.
Keep them on the tablet of miracles.
Withdraw from fine linen and goat's hair
and be prepared to anoint yourself with oil.
My time has come.
There are twenty people in my belly,
there is a magnitude of wings,
there are forty eyes shooting like arrows,
and they will all be born.
All be born in the yellow wind.

I will give suck to all
but they will go hungry,
they will go forth into suffering.
I will fondle each
but it will come to nothing.

They will not nest
for they are the Christs
and each will wave good-bye.

GOD'S BACKSIDE

Cold
like Grandfather's icehouse,
ice forming like a vein
and the trees,
rocks of frozen blood,
and me asking questions of the weather.
And me stupidly observing.
Me swallowing the stone of winter.
Three miles away cars push
by on the highway.
Across the world
bombs drop
in their awful labor.
Ten miles away
the city faints on its lights.
But here
there are only a few houses,
trees, rocks, telephone wires
and the cold punching the earth.
Cold slicing the windowpane
like a razor blade
for God, it seems,
has turned his backside to us,
giving us the dark negative,
the death wing,
until such time

as a flower breaks down the front door
and we cry "Father! Mother!"
and plan their wedding.

JESUS WALKING

When Jesus walked into the wilderness
he carried a man on his back,
at least it had the form of a man,
a fisherman perhaps with a wet nose,
a baker perhaps with flour in his eyes.
The man was dead it seems
and yet he was unkillable.
Jesus carried many men
yet there was only one man —
if indeed it was a man.
There in the wilderness all the leaves
reached out their hands
but Jesus went on by.
The bees beckoned him to their honey
but Jesus went on by.
The boar cut out its heart and offered it
but Jesus went on by
with his heavy burden.
The devil approached and slapped him on the jaw
and Jesus walked on.
The devil made the earth move like an elevator
and Jesus walked on.
The devil built a city of whores,
each in little angel beds,
and Jesus walked on with his burden.
For forty days, for forty nights

Jesus put one foot in front of the other
and the man he carried,
if it was a man,
became heavier and heavier.
He was carrying all the trees of the world
which are one tree.
He was carrying forty moons
which are one moon.
He was carrying all the boots
of all the men in the world
which are one boot.
He was carrying our blood.
One blood.

To pray, Jesus knew,
is to be a man carrying a man.

HURRY UP PLEASE IT'S TIME

What is death, I ask.
What is life, you ask.

I give them both my buttocks,
my two wheels rolling off toward Nirvana.
They are as neat as a wallet,
opening and closing on their coins,
the quarters, the nickels,
straight into the crapper.
Why shouldn't I pull down my pants
and moon at the executioner
as well as paste raisins on my breasts?
Why shouldn't I pull down my pants
and show my little cunny to Tom
and Albert? They wee-wee funny.
I wee-wee like a squaw.
I have ink but no pen, still
I dream that I can piss in God's eye.
I dream I'm a boy with a zipper.
It's so practical, la de dah.
The trouble with being a woman, Skeezix,
is being a little girl in the first place.
Not all the books of the world will change that.
I have swallowed an orange, being woman.
You have swallowed a ruler, being man.
Yet waiting to die we are the same thing.

Jehovah pleasures himself with his axe
before we are both overthrown.
Skeezix, you are me. La de dah.
You grow a beard but our drool is identical.

Forgive us, Father, for we know not.

Today is November 14th, 1972.
I live in Weston, Mass., Middlesex County,
U.S.A., and it rains steadily
in the pond like white puppy eyes.
The pond is waiting for its skin.
The pond is watching for its leather.
The pond is waiting for December and its Novocain.

It begins:

Interrogator:
What can you say of your last seven days?

Anne:
They were tired.

Interrogator:
One day is enough to perfect a man.

Anne:
I watered and fed the plant.

*

My undertaker waits for me.
He is probably twenty-three now,
learning his trade.

He'll stitch up the green,
he'll fasten the bones down
lest they fly away.
I am flying today.
I am not tired today.
I am a motor.
I am cramming in the sugar.
I am running up the hallways.
I am squeezing out the milk.
I am dissecting the dictionary.
I am God, la de dah.
Peanut butter is the American food.
We all eat it, being patriotic.

Ms. Dog is out fighting the dollars,
rolling in a field of bucks.
You've got it made if
you take the wafer,
take some wine,
take some bucks,
the green papery song of the office.
What a jello she could make with it,
the fives, the tens, the twenties,
all in a goo to feed to baby.
Andrew Jackson as an hors d'oeuvre,
la de dah.
I wish I were the U.S. Mint,
turning it all out,
turtle green
and monk black.
Who's that at the podium
in black and white,

blurting into the mike?
Ms. Dog.
Is she spilling her guts?
You bet.
Otherwise they cough . . .
The day is slipping away, why am I
out here, what do they want?
I am sorrowful in November . . .
(no they don't want that,
they want bee stings).
Toot, toot, tootsy don't cry.
Toot, toot, tootsy good-bye.
If you don't get a letter then
you'll know I'm in jail . . .
Remember that, Skeezix,
our first song?

Who's thinking those things?
Ms. Dog! She's out fighting the dollars.

Milk is the American drink.
Oh queen of sorrows,
oh water lady,
place me in your cup
and pull over the clouds
so no one can see.
She don't want no dollars.
She done want a mama.
The white of the white.

Anne says:
This is the rainy season.

I am sorrowful in November.
The kettle is whistling.
I must butter the toast.
And give it jam too.
My kitchen is a heart.
I must feed it oxygen once in a while
and mother the mother.

*

Say the woman is forty-four.
Say she is five seven-and-a-half.
Say her hair is stick color.
Say her eyes are chameleon.
Would you put her in a sack and bury her,
suck her down into the dumb dirt?
Some would.
If not, time will.
Ms. Dog, how much time you got left?
Ms. Dog, when you gonna feel that cold nose?
You better get straight with the Maker
cuz it's a coming, it's a coming!
The cup of coffee is growing and growing
and they're gonna stick your little doll's head
into it and your lungs a gonna get paid
and your clothes a gonna melt.
Hear that, Ms. Dog!
You of the songs,
you of the classroom,
you of the pocketa-pocketa,
you hungry mother,
you spleen baby!

Them angels gonna be cut down like wheat.
Them songs gonna be sliced with a razor.
Them kitchens gonna get a boulder in the belly.
Them phones gonna be torn out at the root.
There's power in the Lord, baby,
and he's gonna turn off the moon.
He's gonna nail you up in a closet
and there'll be no more Atlantic,
no more dreams, no more seeds.
One noon as you walk out to the mailbox
He'll snatch you up —
a woman beside the road like a red mitten.

There's a sack over my head.
I can't see. I'm blind.
The sea collapses. The sun is a bone.
Hi-ho the derry-o,
we all fall down.
If I were a fisherman I could comprehend.
They fish right through the door
and pull eyes from the fire.
They rock upon the daybreak
and amputate the waters.
They are beating the sea,
they are hurting it,
delving down into the inscrutable salt.

*

When mother left the room
and left me in the big black
and sent away my kitty
to be fried in the camps

and took away my blanket
to wash the me out of it
I lay in the soiled cold and prayed.
It was a little jail in which
I was never slapped with kisses.
I was the engine that couldn't.
Cold wigs blew on the trees outside
and car lights flew like roosters
on the ceiling.
Cradle, you are a grave place.

Interrogator:
What color is the devil?

Anne:
Black and blue.

Interrogator:
What goes up the chimney?

Anne:
Fat Lazarus in his red suit.

Forgive us, Father, for we know not.

Ms. Dog prefers to sunbathe nude.
Let the indifferent sky look on.
So what!
Let Mrs. Sewal pull the curtain back,
from her second story.
So what!
Let United Parcel Service see my parcel.
La de dah.

you take it to the book binder.
Pocketa-pocketa.

Once upon a time Ms. Dog was sixty-six.
She had white hair and wrinkles deep as splinters.
Her portrait was nailed up like Christ
and she said of it:
That's when I was forty-two,
down in Rockport with a hat on for the sun,
and Barbara drew a line drawing.
We were, at that moment, drinking vodka
and ginger beer and there was a chill in the air,
although it was July, and she gave me her sweater
to bundle up in. The next summer Skeezix tied
strings in that hat when we were fishing in Maine.
(It had gone into the lake twice.)
Of such moments is happiness made.

Forgive us, Father, for we know not.

Once upon a time we were all born,
popped out like jelly rolls
forgetting our fishdom,
the pleasuring seas,
the country of comfort,
spanked into the oxygens of death,
Good morning life, we say when we wake,
hail mary coffee toast
and we Americans take juice,
a liquid sun going down.
Good morning life.
To wake up is to be born.
To brush your teeth is to be alive.

Sun, you hammer of yellow,
you hat on fire,
you honeysuckle mama,
pour your blonde on me!
Let me laugh for an entire hour
at your supreme being, your Cadillac stuff,
because I've come a long way
from Brussels sprouts.
I've come a long way to peel off my clothes
and lay me down in the grass.
Once only my palms showed.
Once I hung around in my woolly tank suit,
drying my hair in those little meatball curls.
Now I am clothed in gold air with
one dozen halos glistening on my skin.
I am a fortunate lady.
I've gotten out of my pouch
and my teeth are glad
and my heart, that witness,
beats well at the thought.

Oh body, be glad.
You are good goods.

               *

Middle class lady,
you make me smile.
You dig a hole
and come out with a sunburn.
If someone hands you a glass of water
you start constructing a sailboat.
If someone hands you a candy wrapper,

To make a bowel movement is also desirable.
La de dah,
it's all routine.
Often there are wars
yet the shops keep open
and sausages are still fried.
People rub someone.
People copulate
entering each other's blood,
tying each other's tendons in knots,
transplanting their lives into the bed.
It doesn't matter if there are wars,
the business of life continues
unless you're the one that gets it.
Mama, they say, as their intestines
leak out. Even without wars
life is dangerous.
Boats spring leaks.
Cigarettes explode.
The snow could be radioactive.
Cancer could ooze out of the radio.
Who knows?
Ms. Dog stands on the shore
and the sea keeps rocking in
and she wants to talk to God.

Interrogator:
Why talk to God?

Anne:
It's better than playing bridge.

          *

Learning to talk is a complex business.
My daughter's first word was *utta,*
meaning button.
Before there are words
do you dream?
In utero
do you dream?
Who taught you to suck?
And how come?
You don't need to be taught to cry.
The soul presses a button.
Is the cry saying something?
Does it mean *help?*
Or hello?
The cry of a gull is beautiful
and the cry of a crow is ugly
but what I want to know
is whether they mean the same thing.
Somewhere a man sits with indigestion
and he doesn't care.
A woman is in a store buying bracelets
and earrings and she doesn't care.
La de dah.

Forgive us, Father, for we know not.

There are stars and faces.
There is ketchup and guitars.
There is the hand of a small child
when you're crossing the street.
There is the old man's last words:
More light! More light!

Ms. Dog wouldn't give them her buttocks.
She wouldn't moon at *them*.
Just at the killers of the dream.
The bus boys of the soul.
Or at death
who wants to make her a mummy.
And you too!
Wants to stuff her in a cold shoe
and then amputate the foot.
And you too!
La de dah.
What's the point of fighting the dollars
when all you need is a warm bed?
When the dog barks you let him in.
All we need is someone to let us in.
And one other thing:
to consider the lilies in the field.
Of course earth is a stranger,
we pull at its arms
and still it won't speak.
The sea is worse.
It comes in, falling to its knees
but we can't translate the language.
It is only known that they are here to worship,
to worship the terror of the rain,
the mud and all its people,
the body itself,
working like a city,
the night and its slow blood,
the autumn sky, Mary blue.
But more than that,
to worship the question itself,

though the buildings burn
and the big people topple over in a faint.
Bring a flashlight, Ms. Dog,
and look in every corner of the brain
and ask and ask and ask
until the kingdom,
however queer,
will come.

O YE TONGUES

First Psalm

Let there be a God as large as a sunlamp to laugh his heat at you.

Let there be an earth with a form like a jigsaw and let it fit for all of ye.

Let there be the darkness of a darkroom out of the deep. A worm room.

Let there be a God who sees light at the end of a long thin pipe and lets it in.

Let God divide them in half.

Let God share his Hoodsie.

Let the waters divide so that God may wash his face in first light.

Let there be pin holes in the sky in which God puts his little finger.

Let the stars be a heaven of jelly rolls and babies laughing.

Let the light be called Day so that men may grow corn or take busses.

Let there be on the second day dry land so that all men may dry their toes with Cannon towels.

Let God call this earth and feel the grasses rise up like angel hair.

Let there be bananas, cucumbers, prunes, mangoes, beans, rice and candy canes.

Let them seed and reseed.

Let there be seasons so that we may learn the architecture of the sky with eagles, finches, flickers, seagulls.

Let there be seasons so that we may put on twelve coats and shovel snow or take off our skins and bathe in the Carribean.

Let there be seasons so the sky dogs will jump across the sun in December.

Let there be seasons so that the eel may come out of her green cave.

Let there be seasons so that the raccoon may raise his blood level.

Let there be seasons so that the wind may be hoisted for an orange leaf.

Let there be seasons so that the rain will bury many ships.

Let there be seasons so that the miracles will fill our drinking glass with runny gold.

Let there be seasons so that our tongues will be rich in asparagus and limes.

Let there be seasons so that our fires will not forsake us and turn to metal.

Let there be seasons so that a man may close his palm on a woman's breast and bring forth a sweet nipple, a starberry.

Let there be a heaven so that man may outlive his grasses.

Second Psalm

Let Noah build an ark out of the old lady's shoe and fill it with the creatures of the Lord.

Let the ark of salvation have many windows so the creatures of the Lord will marry mouthfuls of oxygen.

Let the ark of salvation do homage to the Lord and notch his belt repeatedly.

Let Anne and Christopher kneel with a buzzard whose mouth will bite her toe so that she may offer it up.

Let Anne and Christopher appear with two robins whose worms are sweet and pink as lipstick.

Let them present a bee, cupped in their palms, zinging the electricity of the Lord out into little yellow Z's.

Let them give praise with a bull whose horns are yellow with history.

Praise the Lord with an ox who grows sweet in heaven and ties the hair ribbons of little girls.

Humble themselves with the fly buzzing like the mother of the engine.

Serve with the ape who tone down the Empire Sate Building and won the maid.

Dedicate an ant who will crawl toward the Lord like the print of this page.

Bless with a sable who bleeds ink across the dresses of ladies of the court.

Bless with a rabbit who comes with a whole sackful of sperm.

Bless with the locust who dances a curtain over the sky and makes the field blind.

Bless with the kingfish who melts down dimes into slim silver beside Frisco.

Rejoice with the day lily for it is born for a day to live by the mailbox and glorify the roadside.

Rejoice with the olive for it gives forth a faithful oil and eaten alone it will grease the mouth and bury the teeth.

Rejoice with a French angelfish which floats by like a jewel glowing like a blue iceberg in the Carribean.

Rejoice with a cottonbush which grows stars and seeds to clothe the multitudes of America.

Rejoice with the sea horse who lives in amusement parks and poems.

Let Anne and Christopher rejoice with the worm who moves into the light like a doll's penis.

Third Psalm

For I am an orphan with two death masks on the mantel and came from the grave of my mama's belly into the commerce of Boston.

For there were only two windows on the city and the buildings ate me.

For I was swaddled in grease wool from my father's company and could not move or ask the time.

For Anne and Christopher were born in my head as I howled at the grave of the roses, the ninety-four rose crèches of my bedroom.

For Christopher, my imaginary brother, my twin holding his baby cock like a minnow.

For I became a *we* and this imaginary *we* became a kind company when the big balloons did not bend over us.

For I could not read or speak and on the long nights I could not turn the moon off or count the lights of cars across the ceiling.

For I lay as pale as flour and drank moon juice from a rubber tip.

For I wet my pants and Christopher told the clock and it ticked like a July cricket and silently moved its spoons.

For I shat and Christopher smiled and said let the air be sweet with your soil.

For I listened to Christopher unless the balloon came and changed my bandage.

For my crotch itched and hands oiled it.

For I lay as single as death. Christopher lay beside me. He was living.

For I lay as stiff as the paper roses and Christopher took a tin basin and bathed me.

For I spoke not but the magician played me tricks of the blood.

For I heard not but for the magician lying beside me playing like a radio.

For I cried then and my little box wiggled with melancholy.

For I was in a boundary of wool and painted boards. Where are we Christopher? Jail, he said.

For the room itself was a box. Four thick walls of roses. A ceiling Christopher found low and menacing.

For I smiled and there was no one to notice. Christopher was asleep. He was making a sea sound.

For I wiggled my fingers but they would not stay. I could not put them in place. They broke out of my mouth.

For I was prodding myself out of my sleep, out the green room. The sleep of the desperate who travel backwards into darkness.

For birth was a disease and Christopher and I invented the cure.

For we swallow magic and we deliver Anne.

Fourth Psalm

Let Christopher and Anne come forth with a pig as bold as an assistant professor. He who comes forth from soil and the subway makes poison sweet.

Let them come forth with a mole who has come from the artificial anus into the light to swallow the sun.

Come forth with a daisy who opens like a hand and wants to be counted for *he loves me*.

Come forth with an orange who will turn its flashlight on and glow in the dark like something holy.

Come forth with a snail who ties and unties his brain within a hard skull. No one sends a letter to the snail.

Let Christopher and Anne come forth with a squid who will come bringing his poison to wash over the Lord like melted licorice.

Come forth with a cauliflower who will plunk herself down beside Him and worry like a white brain.

Come forth with a rose who unfolds like nether lips and is a languid delight.

Come forth with a daffodil who is got up as a ballerina and who dances out into the ancient spring.

Come forth with a dog who is spotted and smiling and holds up his paw for the awful stars.

Come forth with a cockroach large enough to be Franz Kafka (may he rest in peace though locked in his room). Surely all who are locked in boxes of different sizes should have their hands held. Trains and planes should not be locked. One should be allowed to fly out of them and into the Lord's mouth. The Lord is my shepherd, He will swallow me. The Lord is my shepherd, He will allow me back out.

Let Christopher and Anne come forth with a carp who is two-thirds too large to fit anywhere happy.

Come with a leopard who seeps like oil across the branch and has cotton batten for paws.

Come with the Mediterranean on a sunny day where the stars sleep one inch below the surface.

Come with a tree-frog who is more important to the field than Big Ben. He should not be locked in.

Fifth Psalm

For America is a lady rocking on a porch in an unpainted house on an unused road but Anne does not see it.

For America is a librarian in Wichita coughing dust and sharing sourballs with the postman.

For America is Dr. Abraham passing out penicillin and sugar pills to the town of Woolrich, Pennsylvania.

For America is an old man washing his feet in Albion, Michigan. Drying them carefully and then applying Dr. Scholl's foot powder. But Anne does not see it. Anne is locked in.

For America is a reformed burglar turned locksmith who pulls up the shades of his shop at nine A.M. daily (except Sunday when he leaves his phone number on the shop door).

For America is a fat woman dusting a grand piano in English Creek, New Jersey.

For America is a suede glove manufacturer sitting in his large swivel chair feeling the goods and assessing his assets and debits.

For America is a bus driver in Embarrass, Minnesota, clocking the miles and watching the little cardboard suitcases file by.

For America is a land of Commies and Prohibitionists but Anne does not see it. Anne is locked in. The Trotskyites don't see her. The Republicans have never tweaked her chin for she is not there. Anne hides inside folding and unfolding rose after rose. She has no one. She has Christopher. They sit in their room pinching the dolls' noses, poking the dolls' eyes. One time they gave a doll a ride in a fuzzy slipper but that was too far, too far wasn't it. Anne did not dare. She put the slipper with the doll inside it as in a car right into the closet and pushed the door shut.

For America is the headlight man at the Ford plant in Detroit, Michigan, he of the wires, he of the white globe, all day, all day, all year, all his year's headlights, seventy a day, improved by automation but Anne does not.

For America is a miner in Ohio, slipping into the dark hole and bringing forth cat's eyes each night.

For America is only this room . . . there is no useful activity.

For America only your dolls are cheerful.

Sixth Psalm

Let all rejoice with a boa whose twenty feet loosen the tree and the rock and coil like a rubber rope.

Rejoice with the Postmaster General who sits at his desk in Washington and draws faces on the stamps.

Bring forth the vulture who is a meat watcher from the clouds.

Give praise with the spider who builds a city out of her toes.

Rejoice with the Japanese beetle who feasts on rose petals, those mouths of honey.

Rejoice with Peter Pan who flies gold to the crocodile.

Rejoice with the sea otter who floats on her back and carries her young on her tummy.

Give praise with the lobster who is the almighty picker-upper and is still fine to the tongue.

Rejoice with the oyster who lies safely in his hard-nosed shell and who can be eaten alive.

Rejoice with the panda bear who hugs himself.

Rejoice with the roach who is despised among creatures and yet allowed his ugly place.

Rejoice with the anchovy who darts in and out of salads.

Give praise with the barnacle who cements himself to the rock and lets the waves feed him green stuff.

Give praise with the whale who will make a big warm home for Jonah and let him hang his very own pictures up.

Give praise with the grape for lovers will wear them on their toes.

Rejoice with the potato which is a sweet lover and made of angel-mattresses.

Rejoice with broccoli for it is a good bush-of-a-face and goes nicely in the mouth.

Let Christopher and Anne rejoice with Winston Churchill and his hot and cold Blitz.

Let them rejoice with the speedboat that skims by, leaving white lines behind it, making the sea a tennis court for a minute.

Seventh Psalm

No. No. The woman is cheerful, she smiles at her stomach. She has swallowed a bagful of oranges and she is well pleased.

For she has come through the voyage fit and her room carries the little people.

For she has outlived the dates in the back of Fords, she has outlived the penises of her teens to come here, to the married harbor.

For she is the forbidden one, telling time by her ten long fingers.

For she is the dangerous hills and many a climber will be lost on such a passage.

For she is lost from mankind; she is knitting her own hair into a baby shawl.

For she is stuffed by Christopher into a neat package that will not undo until the weeks pass.

For she is a magnitude, she is many. She is each of us patting ourselves dry with a towel.

For she is nourished by darkness.

For she is in the dark room putting bones into place.

For she is clustering the gold and the silver, the minerals and chemicals.

For she is a hoarder, she puts away silks and wools and lips and small white eyes.

For she is seeing the end of her confinement now and is waiting like a stone for the waters.

For the baby crowns and there is a people-dawn in the world.

For the baby lies in its water and blood and there is a people-cry in the world.

For the baby suckles and there is a people made of milk for her to use. There are milk trees to hiss her on. There are milk beds in which to lie and dream of a warm room. There are milk fingers to fold and unfold. There are milk bottoms that are wet and caressed and put into their cotton.

For there are many worlds of milk to walk through under the moon.

For the baby grows and the mother places her giggle-jog on her knee and sings a song of Christopher and Anne.

For the mother sings songs of the baby that knew.

For the mother remembers the baby she was and never locks and twists or puts lonely into a foreign place.

For the baby lives. The mother will die and when she does Christopher will go with her. Christopher who stabbed his kisses and cried up to make two out of one.

Eighth Psalm

Let the chipmunk praise the Lord as he bounds up Jacob's Ladder.

Let the airplane praise the Lord as she flirts with the kingdom.

Let the Good Fairy praise with her heavy bagful of dimes.

Let them praise with a garbage can for all who are cast out.

Praise with a basketball as it enters God's mouth.

Praise with a lemon peel as it floats in the president's drink.

Praise with an ice cube for it will hold up miniature polar bears for a second.

Serve with a sheep for it will crimp the Lord's beard with a curling iron.

Serve with a donkey to carry the worrying angel into Jerusalem.

Rejoice with a Mustang for it will dance down the highway and bump no one.

Appear with a flashlight so the stars will not get tired.

Bring forth a wheel to cart the dead into paradise.

Praise with a fork so that the angels may eat scrambled eggs on Sunday nights.

Come forth with an exit sign so that all those entering will know the way out.

Come forth with a homebody so that she may humble her mops on God's feet.

Come forth with an opera singer so that each concert she may let the moon out of her mouth.

Rejoice with the goldfish for it swallows the sunset from its little glass bowl.

Rejoice with a priest who swallows his collar like a tongue depressor.

Rejoice with a rabbi who combs his beard out like eel grass.

Bring forth a pigeon who will eat popcorn or toenail parings.

Ninth Psalm

For as the baby springs out like a starfish into her million light years Anne sees that she must climb her own mountain.

For as she eats wisdom like the halves of a pear she puts one foot in front of the other. She climbs the dark wing.

For as her child grows Anne grows and there is salt and cantaloupe and molasses for all.

For as Anne walks, the music walks and the family lies down in milk.

For I am not locked up.

For I am placing fist over fist on rock and plunging into the altitude of words. The silence of words.

For the husband sells his rain to God and God is well pleased with His family.

For they fling together against hardness and somewhere, in another room, a light is clicked on by gentle fingers.

For death comes to friends, to parents, to sisters. Death comes with its bagful of pain yet they do not curse the key they were given to hold.

For they open each door and it gives them a new day at the yellow window.

For the child grows to a woman, her breasts coming up like the moon while Anne rubs the peace stone.

For the child starts up her own mountain (not being locked in) and reaches the coastline of grapes.

For Anne and her daughter master the mountain and again and again. Then the child finds a man who opens like the sea.

For that daughter must build her own city and fill it with her own oranges, her own words.

For Anne walked up and up and finally over the years until she was old as the moon and with its naggy voice.

For Anne had climbed over eight mountains and saw the children washing the tiny statues in the square.

For Anne sat down with the blood of a hammer and built a tombstone for herself and Christopher sat beside her and was well pleased with their red shadow.

For they hung up a picture of a rat and the rat smiled and held out his hand.

For the rat was blessed on that mountain. He was given a white bath.

For the milk in the skies sank down upon them and tucked them in.

For God did not forsake them but put the blood angel to look after them until such time as they would enter their star.

For the sky dogs jumped out and shoveled snow upon us and we lay in our quiet blood.

For God was as large as a sunlamp and laughed his heat at us and therefore we did not cringe at the death hole.